Table of Contents

Chapter 1: Introduction to AI Ethics

Understanding the Importance of Ethics in AI

In today's rapidly advancing technological landscape, the integration of artificial intelligence (AI) into various industries has become increasingly prevalent. As professionals and innovators in the field of AI ethics and regulation, it is crucial to understand the importance of ethics in AI. Ethics play a fundamental role in ensuring that AI systems are developed and utilized in a responsible and ethical manner, with consideration for the potential impact on individuals, society, and the environment.

Ethics in AI encompasses a wide range of considerations, including fairness, transparency, accountability, and privacy. By adhering to ethical principles, professionals and innovators can help to mitigate the risks associated with AI, such as bias, discrimination, and unintended consequences. Ethical AI practices also foster trust and credibility among stakeholders, including users, regulators, and the general public, which is essential for the long-term success and sustainability of AI technologies.

One of the key reasons why ethics is important in AI is to ensure that AI systems are developed and deployed in a way that aligns with societal values and norms. By considering ethical implications early in the design and development process, professionals and innovators can help to prevent harm and promote the well-being of individuals and communities. Ethical AI practices also support compliance with regulations and standards, which are increasingly being implemented to govern the use of AI in various industries.

Furthermore, ethical considerations in AI can help to address issues related to bias and discrimination, which have been a significant concern in the development and deployment of AI systems. By promoting fairness and inclusivity in AI technologies, professionals and innovators can help to reduce the negative impact of bias on marginalized groups and ensure that AI systems are designed to benefit all individuals equally. Ethical AI practices also encourage transparency and accountability, enabling stakeholders to understand how AI systems work and how decisions are made.

In conclusion, understanding the importance of ethics in AI is essential for professionals and innovators working in the field of AI ethics and regulation. By prioritizing ethical considerations in the design, development, and deployment of AI systems, professionals can help to ensure that AI technologies are developed and utilized in a responsible and ethical manner. Ultimately, ethical AI practices not only promote trust and credibility among stakeholders but also help to address complex ethical challenges and mitigate the risks associated with AI technologies.

Overview of AI Regulations

In the rapidly evolving field of artificial intelligence (AI), regulations play a crucial role in ensuring the ethical development and deployment of AI technologies. This subchapter provides an overview of the current landscape of AI regulations, focusing on key principles and guidelines that professionals and innovators in the AI ethics and regulation niches need to be aware of. By understanding and adhering to these regulations, individuals and organizations can navigate the complex ethical landscape of AI while promoting responsible and sustainable innovation.

One of the primary objectives of AI regulations is to protect the rights and well-being of individuals affected by AI technologies. This includes ensuring the privacy and security of personal data, as well as preventing discrimination and bias in AI decision-making processes. Regulations also address the accountability and transparency of AI systems, requiring developers to clearly document and explain the algorithms and data sources used in their applications. By upholding these principles, professionals and innovators can build trust with stakeholders and demonstrate a commitment to ethical AI practices.

In addition to protecting individuals, AI regulations also aim to foster competition and innovation in the marketplace. By establishing guidelines for fair competition and intellectual property rights, regulations help prevent monopolies and promote a level playing field for companies developing AI technologies. Regulations also address the potential social and economic impacts of AI, such as job displacement and income inequality, by encouraging responsible AI development and deployment that considers the broader societal implications.

The regulatory landscape for AI is constantly evolving as technology advances and ethical concerns continue to emerge. Professionals and innovators in the AI ethics and regulation niches must stay informed about the latest developments in AI regulations at both the national and international levels. This includes monitoring changes in legislation, guidelines, and best practices related to AI, as well as actively participating in policy discussions and regulatory initiatives to shape the future of AI governance.

By proactively engaging with AI regulations and embracing ethical principles in their work, professionals and innovators can contribute to a more responsible and sustainable AI ecosystem. This subchapter serves as a starting point for understanding the key considerations and challenges in navigating the ethical landscape of AI regulations, empowering individuals and organizations to make informed decisions and drive positive change in the field of AI ethics and regulation.

The Ethical Landscape of Artificial Intelligence

The Ethical Landscape of Artificial Intelligence is a complex and rapidly evolving field that raises important questions about how we should use and regulate AI technologies. As professionals and innovators in the AI industry, it is crucial that we navigate this landscape thoughtfully and ethically to ensure that AI is used in ways that benefit society as a whole.

One of the key ethical considerations in AI is the issue of bias. AI algorithms are only as good as the data they are trained on, and if that data is biased, the AI system will perpetuate those biases. This can lead to discriminatory outcomes in areas such as hiring, lending, and criminal justice. As professionals, we must take steps to identify and mitigate bias in our AI systems to ensure fair and equitable outcomes.

Another important ethical consideration in AI is transparency. AI systems can be opaque and difficult to understand, making it challenging to hold them accountable for their decisions. As professionals, we have a responsibility to ensure that AI systems are transparent and explainable, so that users can understand how decisions are being made and challenge them if necessary.

Privacy is also a critical ethical consideration in AI. AI systems often rely on vast amounts of personal data to make decisions, raising concerns about how that data is collected, stored, and used. As professionals, we must prioritize the protection of user privacy and ensure that AI systems are designed with privacy in mind, following best practices and regulations to safeguard sensitive information.

Finally, as professionals and innovators in the AI industry, we must consider the broader societal impacts of our work. AI technologies have the potential to bring about significant social and economic changes, and it is important that we consider the ethical implications of these changes. By engaging with stakeholders, including policymakers, advocacy groups, and the public, we can ensure that AI is developed and deployed in ways that benefit society as a whole.

Chapter 2: Ethical Frameworks in AI

Utilitarianism and AI Ethics

Utilitarianism is a moral theory that emphasizes the greatest good for the greatest number. When it comes to the ethical considerations surrounding artificial intelligence (AI), utilitarianism can be a useful framework for evaluating the impact of AI technologies on society. As professionals and innovators in the field of AI ethics and regulation, it is important to understand how utilitarianism can inform our decision-making processes.

One of the key principles of utilitarianism is the idea of maximizing overall well-being. When applying this principle to AI ethics, professionals and innovators must consider the potential benefits and harms that AI technologies may bring to society as a whole. This requires a thoughtful analysis of the potential consequences of AI applications, including issues such as privacy, bias, and job displacement.

Utilitarianism also emphasizes the importance of considering the interests of all stakeholders when making ethical decisions. In the context of AI ethics, this means taking into account the perspectives of not only developers and users of AI technologies, but also those who may be impacted by these technologies in indirect ways. By engaging with a diverse range of stakeholders, professionals and innovators can ensure that their ethical decisions are informed by a comprehensive understanding of the potential risks and benefits of AI.

Furthermore, utilitarianism encourages professionals and innovators to prioritize the well-being of society as a whole over the interests of any individual or group. This can be particularly challenging in the context of AI ethics, where competing interests and values may come into play. By adopting a utilitarian approach, professionals and innovators can strive to make decisions that maximize the overall well-being of society, even if it means sacrificing the interests of some individuals or groups.

In conclusion, utilitarianism can provide a valuable framework for navigating the ethical landscape of AI. By emphasizing the greatest good for the greatest number and considering the interests of all stakeholders, professionals and innovators can make more informed and ethical decisions when developing and regulating AI technologies. As the field of AI continues to evolve, it is essential for professionals and innovators to engage with ethical theories such as utilitarianism in order to promote the responsible and beneficial use of AI for society as a whole.

Deontology and AI Decision Making

In the field of artificial intelligence (AI), decision-making processes are becoming increasingly complex as technology continues to advance. One key ethical framework that is often used to guide AI decision-making is deontology. Deontology is a philosophical approach that focuses on the inherent moral duties and obligations that individuals and, in this case, AI systems have.

When it comes to AI decision-making, deontology emphasizes the importance of following ethical principles and rules, rather than focusing solely on the consequences of actions. This means that AI systems must be programmed to adhere to certain moral principles and guidelines, even if doing so may not always lead to the best outcomes. For professionals and innovators working in the field of AI ethics and regulation, understanding deontology and its implications for AI decision-making is crucial.

One of the key challenges of applying deontological principles to AI decision-making is defining what those principles should be. Unlike humans, AI systems do not have intrinsic moral values or intuitions to guide their actions. This means that professionals and innovators must carefully consider which ethical principles to program into AI systems and how to ensure that they are applied consistently and fairly.

Another important consideration when it comes to deontology and AI decision-making is the issue of accountability. If an AI system makes a decision that results in harm or unethical behavior, who is ultimately responsible? Professionals and innovators must grapple with questions of liability and oversight to ensure that AI systems are held accountable for their actions.

Overall, understanding the role of deontology in AI decision-making is essential for professionals and innovators working in the field of AI ethics and regulation. By carefully considering ethical principles and guidelines, and ensuring that AI systems are programmed to adhere to these principles, professionals can help to ensure that AI technology is developed and deployed in a responsible and ethical manner.

Virtue Ethics in Artificial Intelligence

Virtue ethics is a philosophical approach that focuses on the character traits and moral virtues of individuals rather than on rules or consequences. In the context of artificial intelligence (AI), virtue ethics can provide valuable insights into how AI systems should be designed, developed, and deployed. By emphasizing the importance of cultivating virtuous traits such as honesty, compassion, and fairness in AI systems, professionals and innovators can create AI technologies that are not only technically proficient but also ethically sound.

One of the key principles of virtue ethics is the idea of striving for excellence in all areas of life. In the context of AI, this means designing systems that prioritize accuracy, transparency, and accountability. By setting high ethical standards for AI technologies, professionals and innovators can help ensure that these systems operate in a manner that is consistent with ethical principles and values. This can help to build trust and confidence in AI technologies among users and stakeholders.

Another important aspect of virtue ethics in AI is the concept of phronesis, or practical wisdom. This involves the ability to make sound ethical judgments in complex and uncertain situations. In the rapidly evolving field of AI, professionals and innovators must be able to navigate a wide range of ethical challenges and dilemmas. By cultivating phronesis in their approach to AI development and deployment, professionals can make more informed and ethical decisions that take into account the broader societal impacts of their work.

Virtue ethics also emphasizes the importance of empathy and compassion in ethical decision-making. In the context of AI, this means considering the potential impacts of AI technologies on individuals and communities, and taking steps to mitigate any negative consequences. By prioritizing empathy and compassion in their work, professionals and innovators can help ensure that AI technologies are developed and deployed in a way that respects the dignity and rights of all individuals.

Overall, virtue ethics can provide a valuable framework for guiding ethical decision-making in the field of AI. By focusing on the character traits and moral virtues that should inform the development and deployment of AI technologies, professionals and innovators can create systems that are not only technically proficient but also ethically robust. By incorporating the principles of excellence, practical wisdom, empathy, and compassion into their work, professionals can help ensure that AI technologies contribute to a more just and equitable society.

Chapter 3: Ethical Considerations in AI Development
Bias and Fairness in AI Algorithms

Bias and fairness in AI algorithms are complex and critical issues that must be carefully considered by professionals and innovators in the field of AI ethics and regulation. As artificial intelligence systems become increasingly prevalent in various industries, ensuring that these algorithms are free from bias and promote fairness is essential to uphold ethical standards and prevent harm to individuals and communities.

One of the key challenges in addressing bias in AI algorithms is the inherent biases that can be present in the data used to train these systems. Data sets may reflect existing societal prejudices and inequalities, leading to biased outcomes in AI applications. Professionals and innovators must carefully evaluate the data sources and methodologies used in developing AI algorithms to identify and mitigate potential biases that could impact the fairness of the system.

In addition to addressing bias in data sets, professionals and innovators must also consider the potential for bias to be introduced at various stages of the AI algorithm development process. Biases can be unintentionally introduced through the selection of features, the design of algorithms, or the interpretation of results. It is essential for professionals to be aware of these potential sources of bias and implement strategies to promote fairness and mitigate harm.

Transparency and accountability are key principles that can help address bias and promote fairness in AI algorithms. By making AI systems more transparent and understandable to users, stakeholders, and regulators, professionals can increase trust in the technology and ensure that decisions made by AI algorithms are fair and unbiased. Additionally, establishing mechanisms for accountability and oversight can help identify and address biases in AI systems before they cause harm to individuals or communities.

Overall, addressing bias and promoting fairness in AI algorithms is a complex and ongoing process that requires a multidisciplinary approach. Professionals and innovators in the field of AI ethics and regulation must work together to develop best practices, guidelines, and tools to ensure that AI algorithms are free from bias and promote fairness in decision-making processes. By prioritizing ethical considerations and transparency in the development and deployment of AI systems, professionals can help build a more just and equitable future for all.

Transparency and Accountability in AI Systems

Transparency and accountability are crucial aspects of ensuring the ethical development and deployment of AI systems. In the fast-paced world of artificial intelligence, it is essential for professionals and innovators to prioritize these principles to maintain public trust and confidence in AI technologies. Transparency refers to the openness and clarity of AI systems, including how they are designed, trained, and implemented. This transparency allows stakeholders to understand the decision-making processes of AI systems and to identify any biases or errors that may arise.

Accountability, on the other hand, involves taking responsibility for the actions and outcomes of AI systems. It is important for professionals and innovators to be accountable for the ethical implications of their AI technologies, including any harm or bias that may result from their use. Accountability also includes being transparent about how decisions are made within AI systems, as well as providing avenues for recourse in cases of error or harm.

One way to promote transparency and accountability in AI systems is through the use of explainable AI (XAI) techniques. XAI methods aim to make AI systems more interpretable and understandable to humans, allowing stakeholders to trace the decision-making processes and identify potential biases or errors. By incorporating XAI techniques into AI systems, professionals and innovators can enhance transparency and accountability, ultimately fostering trust and confidence in AI technologies.

Another important aspect of promoting transparency and accountability in AI systems is through the development of ethical guidelines and regulations. By adhering to ethical principles and legal requirements, professionals and innovators can ensure that their AI technologies are used in a responsible and ethical manner. This includes being transparent about data collection and usage, as well as establishing mechanisms for accountability and oversight.

In conclusion, transparency and accountability are essential principles for professionals and innovators working in the field of AI ethics and regulation. By prioritizing these principles, stakeholders can build trust and confidence in AI technologies, while also ensuring that their use remains ethical and responsible. Through the use of explainable AI techniques and adherence to ethical guidelines and regulations, professionals and innovators can navigate the ethical landscape of AI with integrity and transparency.

Privacy and Data Protection in AI

Privacy and data protection are crucial considerations in the development and deployment of artificial intelligence (AI) technologies. As AI systems continue to advance and become more prevalent in our daily lives, it is essential for professionals and innovators in the field to prioritize the protection of individuals' privacy and personal data.

One of the key challenges in ensuring privacy and data protection in AI is the vast amount of data that is required to train and operate AI systems. This data often contains sensitive and personal information, making it essential to implement robust measures to safeguard against unauthorized access or misuse. Professionals and innovators must carefully consider how they collect, store, and process data to minimize the risk of privacy breaches and ensure compliance with regulations such as the General Data Protection Regulation (GDPR).

Furthermore, the use of AI in decision-making processes raises concerns about the potential for bias and discrimination. Professionals and innovators must be aware of the ethical implications of using AI algorithms that may inadvertently perpetuate existing biases or lead to discriminatory outcomes. By implementing transparency and accountability mechanisms, such as algorithm audits and bias mitigation strategies, professionals can help mitigate these risks and ensure that AI systems operate fairly and ethically.

In addition to protecting individuals' privacy and addressing biases, professionals and innovators must also consider the broader societal impacts of AI technologies. The widespread adoption of AI has the potential to transform industries and economies, but it also raises questions about the implications for privacy, security, and human rights. By engaging with stakeholders and fostering open dialogue about the ethical implications of AI, professionals can help shape policies and regulations that protect the public interest while promoting innovation and growth.

In conclusion, privacy and data protection are essential considerations for professionals and innovators working in the field of AI ethics and regulation. By prioritizing the protection of individuals' privacy, addressing biases and discrimination, and considering the broader societal impacts of AI technologies, professionals can help ensure that AI systems are developed and deployed in a responsible and ethical manner. By navigating the ethical landscape of AI with a focus on privacy and data protection, professionals can help build a future where AI technologies benefit society while upholding fundamental ethical principles.

Chapter 4: Ethical Decision Making in AI

Identifying Ethical Dilemmas in AI Projects

In the fast-paced world of artificial intelligence (AI), professionals and innovators are constantly faced with ethical dilemmas that arise during the development and implementation of AI projects. Identifying these dilemmas is crucial in order to navigate the ethical landscape of AI effectively. In this subchapter, we will explore how to recognize ethical dilemmas in AI projects and address them in a responsible and ethical manner.

One common ethical dilemma in AI projects is the issue of bias. Bias can be present in the data used to train AI algorithms, leading to discriminatory outcomes. It is important for professionals and innovators to be aware of bias in AI projects and take steps to mitigate it. This may involve carefully selecting and preprocessing data, as well as regularly monitoring and auditing AI systems for bias.

Another ethical dilemma in AI projects is the potential impact on privacy and data security. AI systems often require vast amounts of data to operate effectively, raising concerns about the potential misuse or unauthorized access to sensitive information. Professionals and innovators must consider the ethical implications of data collection and storage in AI projects, and implement robust privacy and security measures to protect user data.

A third ethical dilemma in AI projects is the issue of transparency and accountability. AI systems can be complex and opaque, making it difficult to understand how they reach decisions or predictions. This lack of transparency can lead to mistrust and skepticism among users and stakeholders. Professionals and innovators must prioritize transparency in AI projects, providing clear explanations of how AI systems work and ensuring accountability for their outcomes.

In conclusion, identifying ethical dilemmas in AI projects is essential for professionals and innovators working in the field of AI ethics and regulation. By recognizing and addressing these dilemmas, we can ensure that AI technology is developed and deployed in a responsible and ethical manner. By taking proactive steps to mitigate bias, protect privacy and data security, and promote transparency and accountability, we can navigate the ethical landscape of AI with confidence and integrity.

Ethical Decision-Making Models for AI Professionals

In the rapidly evolving field of artificial intelligence (AI), ethical decision-making is becoming increasingly important. As AI professionals and innovators, it is crucial to consider the ethical implications of the technologies we develop and deploy. This subchapter will explore various ethical decision-making models that can help guide AI professionals in navigating the complex ethical landscape of their work.

One ethical decision-making model that is commonly used in the field of AI is the principle-based approach. This approach involves identifying and applying a set of ethical principles or values to guide decision-making. For example, AI professionals may consider principles such as transparency, accountability, and fairness when designing and implementing AI systems. By applying these principles, AI professionals can ensure that their work aligns with ethical standards and values.

Another ethical decision-making model that AI professionals can utilize is the consequentialist approach. This approach involves evaluating the potential consequences of a decision or action and choosing the course of action that will result in the greatest overall good. When applying the consequentialist approach to AI development, professionals must consider the potential impacts of their work on society, individuals, and the environment. By prioritizing positive outcomes and minimizing harm, AI professionals can make ethical decisions that benefit the greater good.

In addition to principle-based and consequentialist approaches, AI professionals can also consider the virtue ethics approach to ethical decision-making. This approach involves focusing on the character traits or virtues that individuals should cultivate in order to make ethical decisions. For example, AI professionals may strive to develop virtues such as honesty, integrity, and empathy in order to guide their decision-making processes. By embodying these virtues, AI professionals can make ethical decisions that reflect their commitment to ethical values and principles.

Overall, ethical decision-making models provide AI professionals with a framework for navigating the complex ethical landscape of their work. By considering principles, consequences, and virtues, AI professionals can make informed and ethical decisions that uphold the values of transparency, accountability, and fairness. As the field of AI continues to advance, it is essential for professionals and innovators to prioritize ethical considerations in their work in order to ensure the responsible development and deployment of AI technologies.

Case Studies in Ethical AI Decision Making

In this subchapter, we delve into case studies that illustrate ethical decision-making in the realm of Artificial Intelligence (AI). These real-world examples provide valuable insights into the challenges and complexities faced by professionals and innovators working in AI ethics and regulation. By examining these cases, we can better understand the implications of AI technology and the importance of ethical considerations in its development and deployment.

One such case study involves a healthcare AI system that was designed to assist doctors in diagnosing patients. The system was trained on a large dataset of medical records and was touted as a way to improve accuracy and efficiency in diagnosing illnesses. However, concerns arose when it was discovered that the system was biased towards certain demographics, leading to inaccurate diagnoses for certain groups of patients. This case highlights the importance of ensuring that AI systems are trained on diverse and representative datasets to avoid perpetuating biases in decision-making.

Another case study focuses on a financial institution that implemented an AI algorithm to automate loan approval processes. The algorithm was designed to assess loan applications based on various factors such as credit history and income. However, it was later revealed that the algorithm was systematically discriminating against applicants from marginalized communities, leading to inequitable outcomes. This case underscores the need for transparency and accountability in the design and implementation of AI systems to prevent discriminatory practices.

In a third case study, we explore the ethical considerations surrounding the use of AI in law enforcement. A predictive policing system was deployed in a city to identify areas at high risk for crime based on historical data. While the system was intended to help allocate resources more effectively, it raised concerns about privacy and surveillance, as well as the potential for reinforcing existing biases in policing practices. This case raises important questions about the ethical implications of using AI in sensitive domains such as law enforcement and the need for robust oversight mechanisms to prevent abuse.

By examining these case studies, professionals and innovators in the field of AI ethics and regulation can gain valuable insights into the ethical challenges and considerations that arise in the development and deployment of AI technology. These examples serve as cautionary tales and provide a framework for approaching ethical decision-making in the increasingly complex landscape of AI. Ultimately, by learning from these cases, we can work towards creating more responsible and ethical AI systems that benefit society as a whole.

Chapter 5: Regulatory Frameworks for AI
Overview of Global AI Regulations

The landscape of artificial intelligence (AI) is rapidly evolving, with new technologies and applications emerging at an unprecedented pace. As AI becomes increasingly integrated into various aspects of our lives, it is essential to establish clear and comprehensive regulations to ensure that these technologies are developed and deployed in a responsible and ethical manner. In this subchapter, we will provide an overview of the current global AI regulations and how they impact professionals and innovators in the field of AI ethics and regulation.

One of the key challenges in regulating AI is the lack of a unified approach across different countries and regions. While some countries have developed robust regulatory frameworks to govern the development and deployment of AI technologies, others have yet to establish clear guidelines. This lack of consistency can create confusion and uncertainty for professionals and innovators working in the field of AI ethics and regulation, as they navigate the complex web of regulations that govern AI technologies.

In the European Union, the General Data Protection Regulation (GDPR) has had a significant impact on the development and deployment of AI technologies. The GDPR sets strict guidelines for the collection and processing of personal data, which has implications for AI applications that rely on large datasets. Professionals and innovators working in the EU must ensure that their AI technologies comply with the GDPR to avoid potential legal and ethical consequences.

In the United States, AI regulation is more fragmented, with different federal agencies overseeing various aspects of AI development and deployment. The Federal Trade Commission (FTC) and the National Institute of Standards and Technology (NIST) have both issued guidelines for the ethical use of AI technologies, but there is still a lack of comprehensive federal regulation. This fragmented approach can create challenges for professionals and innovators in the field of AI ethics and regulation, as they navigate the complex regulatory landscape.

Overall, navigating the global AI regulations requires a deep understanding of the legal and ethical considerations that govern the development and deployment of AI technologies. Professionals and innovators working in the field of AI ethics and regulation must stay informed about the latest regulatory developments and trends to ensure that their AI technologies comply with the highest ethical standards. By staying up to date on global AI regulations, professionals and innovators can help shape the future of AI in a responsible and ethical manner.

Compliance with AI Ethics Standards

As professionals and innovators in the field of AI ethics and regulation, it is crucial to understand and comply with the ethical standards set forth in the industry. Compliance with AI ethics standards ensures that AI technologies are developed and deployed in a responsible and ethical manner, prioritizing the well-being of individuals and society as a whole.

One of the key principles of compliance with AI ethics standards is transparency. It is essential for professionals and innovators to be transparent about the data sources, algorithms, and decision-making processes used in AI systems. Transparency builds trust with stakeholders and allows for accountability in the event of ethical concerns or issues arising from AI technologies.

Another important aspect of compliance with AI ethics standards is fairness and non-discrimination. Professionals and innovators must ensure that AI systems do not perpetuate biases or discriminate against individuals based on race, gender, age, or other protected characteristics.

Fairness in AI systems can be achieved through careful data collection, algorithm design, and testing for bias before deployment.

In addition to transparency and fairness, compliance with AI ethics standards also involves ensuring the security and privacy of individuals' data. Professionals and innovators must prioritize data protection and implement robust security measures to safeguard sensitive information collected by AI systems. Respecting individuals' privacy rights is crucial for maintaining trust and ethical standards in the development and deployment of AI technologies.

Overall, compliance with AI ethics standards is essential for professionals and innovators to navigate the ethical landscape of AI responsibly. By prioritizing transparency, fairness, security, and privacy in the development and deployment of AI technologies, professionals can ensure that AI systems benefit society while upholding ethical standards and values. It is imperative for professionals and innovators to stay informed about evolving AI ethics standards and regulations to ensure compliance and ethical practice in the field of AI.

Impact of Regulations on AI Innovation

In the rapidly evolving landscape of artificial intelligence (AI) innovation, regulations play a crucial role in shaping the ethical framework within which these technologies operate. The impact of regulations on AI innovation cannot be overstated, as they serve to provide guidance on how AI systems should be developed, deployed, and utilized in a responsible and transparent manner. For professionals and innovators working in the field of AI ethics and regulation, understanding the implications of these regulations is essential for ensuring that their work aligns with ethical standards and legal requirements.

One of the key ways in which regulations impact AI innovation is by setting standards for data privacy and security. As AI systems rely on vast amounts of data to function effectively, regulations such as the General Data Protection Regulation (GDPR) in Europe and the Health Insurance Portability and Accountability Act (HIPAA) in the United States help to ensure that personal and sensitive information is handled in a secure and ethical manner. By adhering to these regulations, professionals and innovators can build trust with users and stakeholders, ultimately fostering greater acceptance and adoption of AI technologies.

Furthermore, regulations also play a role in addressing issues of bias and discrimination within AI systems. As AI technologies are trained on datasets that may contain biases, regulations such as the Algorithmic Accountability Act in the United States and the AI Ethics Guidelines in Europe aim to promote fairness and transparency in AI decision-making processes. By incorporating principles of fairness and accountability into their work, professionals and innovators can help mitigate the risks of bias and discrimination in AI systems, thereby fostering greater social equity and justice.

In addition to data privacy, security, and bias, regulations also impact AI innovation by addressing issues of accountability and transparency. Regulations such as the AI Act in Europe and the Algorithmic Transparency and Accountability Act in the United States require that AI systems be designed in a way that enables users to understand how decisions are made and hold developers accountable for the outcomes of these systems. By embracing principles of transparency and accountability, professionals and innovators can build trust with users and regulators, ultimately fostering a more ethical and responsible AI ecosystem.

In conclusion, the impact of regulations on AI innovation is profound and far-reaching. By setting standards for data privacy and security, addressing issues of bias and discrimination, and promoting accountability and transparency, regulations help to shape the ethical landscape within which AI technologies operate. For professionals and innovators working in the field of AI ethics and regulation, understanding and adhering to these regulations is essential for ensuring that their work aligns with ethical standards and legal requirements, ultimately fostering greater trust, acceptance, and adoption of AI technologies.

Chapter 6: Ethical Challenges in AI Research and Development

Ethical Issues in AI Research

In the rapidly evolving field of artificial intelligence (AI), researchers and professionals are constantly faced with ethical dilemmas that must be carefully navigated. This subchapter, "Ethical Issues in AI Research," delves into some of the key ethical considerations that arise in the development and implementation of AI technologies. For professionals and innovators working in the niche of AI ethics and regulation, it is crucial to be aware of these ethical issues and to have strategies in place to address them effectively.

One of the primary ethical issues in AI research is the potential for bias in algorithms. AI systems are only as good as the data they are trained on, and if this data is biased or incomplete, the AI system will produce biased results. This can have serious consequences, particularly in areas such as hiring, lending, and criminal justice, where biased algorithms can perpetuate discrimination and inequality. Professionals and innovators must be vigilant in identifying and mitigating bias in AI systems to ensure fair and equitable outcomes.

Another ethical issue in AI research is the question of accountability and transparency. AI systems are often complex and opaque, making it difficult to understand how they arrive at their decisions. This lack of transparency can be problematic, particularly in high-stakes applications such as autonomous vehicles or medical diagnosis. Professionals and innovators must prioritize transparency in AI systems, ensuring that they are accountable for their decisions and that users understand how these decisions are made.

Privacy is also a significant ethical issue in AI research. AI systems often rely on vast amounts of personal data to function effectively, raising concerns about data security and privacy rights. Professionals and innovators must take steps to protect user privacy and ensure that data is handled responsibly. This may involve implementing robust data protection measures, obtaining informed consent from users, and being transparent about how data is used and shared.

Finally, the ethical implications of AI research extend to broader societal concerns, such as job displacement and the impact on human autonomy. As AI technologies continue to advance, there is a growing concern about the potential for widespread job loss and economic disruption. Professionals and innovators must consider the social and ethical implications of AI research, working to ensure that these technologies are developed and deployed in a way that benefits society as a whole. By addressing these ethical issues head-on, professionals and innovators can help to ensure that AI technologies are developed and used in a responsible and ethical manner.

Responsible AI Development Practices

In the rapidly evolving field of artificial intelligence (AI), it is imperative for professionals and innovators to prioritize responsible AI development practices. These practices ensure that AI technologies are developed and deployed in an ethical manner that respects human rights and values. In this subchapter, we will explore key principles and guidelines for responsible AI development that can help navigate the complex ethical landscape of AI.

One important aspect of responsible AI development is transparency. Professionals and innovators should strive to make their AI algorithms and decision-making processes transparent and understandable to users. This transparency can help build trust with stakeholders and ensure that AI systems are used in a fair and accountable manner. By providing clear explanations of how AI technologies work and how they make decisions, developers can empower users to make informed choices and hold AI systems accountable for their actions.

Another crucial principle of responsible AI development is fairness. AI systems should be designed and implemented in a way that promotes fairness and prevents bias and discrimination. Professionals and innovators should carefully consider the potential impact of their AI technologies on different groups of people and ensure that their systems do not reinforce existing inequalities or create new forms of discrimination. By prioritizing fairness in AI development, developers can help build a more inclusive and equitable society.

In addition to transparency and fairness, professionals and innovators should also prioritize privacy and data protection in their AI development practices. AI technologies often rely on large amounts of personal data to function effectively, and it is essential that this data is handled responsibly and in accordance with relevant privacy laws and regulations. By implementing robust data protection measures and respecting users' privacy rights, developers can help build trust with stakeholders and ensure that AI systems are used in a way that respects individuals' rights and freedoms.

Overall, responsible AI development practices are essential for ensuring that AI technologies are developed and deployed in a way that upholds ethical values and promotes the common good. By prioritizing transparency, fairness, and privacy in their AI development processes, professionals and innovators can help navigate the complex ethical landscape of AI and build a more ethical and sustainable future for AI technologies.

Ethical Guidelines for AI Innovators

In the rapidly evolving field of artificial intelligence (AI), it is essential for professionals and innovators to adhere to ethical guidelines to ensure that their work is aligned with the values and principles of society. This subchapter will outline some key ethical guidelines for AI innovators to consider as they develop and deploy AI technologies.

First and foremost, AI innovators must prioritize transparency in their work. This means being open and honest about the capabilities and limitations of their AI systems, as well as how they are being used. Transparency builds trust with users and stakeholders, and helps to prevent the spread of misinformation and bias in AI systems.

Secondly, AI innovators must prioritize fairness and equity in the design and deployment of their AI technologies. This means ensuring that AI systems do not discriminate against individuals or groups based on factors such as race, gender, or socioeconomic status. It also means actively working to mitigate bias in AI systems through techniques such as data cleaning and algorithm auditing.

Additionally, AI innovators must prioritize accountability in their work. This means taking responsibility for the outcomes of their AI systems, and being prepared to address any negative impacts that may arise. By holding themselves accountable, AI innovators can help to build a culture of ethical behavior in the field of AI.

Furthermore, AI innovators must prioritize privacy and data security in their work. This means taking steps to protect the personal data of users and stakeholders, and ensuring that it is not misused or exposed to unauthorized parties. By prioritizing privacy and data security, AI innovators can help to build trust with users and stakeholders, and ensure that their AI systems are used responsibly.

In conclusion, ethical guidelines are essential for AI innovators to navigate the complex landscape of AI technologies. By prioritizing transparency, fairness, accountability, privacy, and data security in their work, AI innovators can help to ensure that their AI systems are aligned with the values and principles of society. By following these guidelines, AI innovators can contribute to the responsible development and deployment of AI technologies, and help to build a more ethical and sustainable future for the field of AI.

Chapter 7: The Future of AI Ethics
Emerging Trends in AI Ethics

As AI technology continues to advance at a rapid pace, the ethical implications of its use are becoming increasingly complex and important. In this subchapter, we will explore some of the emerging trends in AI ethics that professionals and innovators in the field should be aware of.

One of the key trends in AI ethics is the growing emphasis on transparency and explainability in AI algorithms. As AI systems are being used in more critical applications such as healthcare and finance, there is a growing demand for algorithms to be transparent and able to explain their decisions. This trend is driven by concerns about bias and discrimination in AI systems, as well as the need for accountability and trust in AI technology.

Another important trend in AI ethics is the increasing recognition of the need for diversity and inclusivity in AI development. Research has shown that AI systems can perpetuate and even exacerbate existing biases and inequalities if they are not developed with diverse perspectives and input. Professionals and innovators in the field are now being urged to take a more inclusive approach to AI development, involving a diverse range of stakeholders in the design and testing of AI systems.

A third trend in AI ethics is the growing focus on data privacy and security. As AI systems become more sophisticated and powerful, they are also becoming more reliant on vast amounts of data. This trend raises important questions about how data is collected, stored, and used in AI systems, as well as the potential risks to privacy and security that may arise from the misuse of data.

In conclusion, the field of AI ethics is constantly evolving, with new trends and challenges emerging all the time. Professionals and innovators in the field must stay informed about these trends and work together to address the ethical implications of AI technology. By staying ahead of these trends and taking a proactive approach to AI ethics, we can ensure that AI technology is used responsibly and ethically for the benefit of society as a whole.

Ethical Implications of Advanced AI Technologies

In the rapidly evolving landscape of artificial intelligence (AI) technologies, the ethical implications of advanced AI systems are becoming increasingly complex and nuanced. As professionals and innovators in the field of AI ethics and regulation, it is crucial to understand and navigate these ethical challenges in order to ensure that AI technologies are developed and deployed in a responsible and ethical manner.

One of the key ethical implications of advanced AI technologies is the potential for bias and discrimination in AI systems. AI algorithms are only as good as the data they are trained on, and if the training data is biased or incomplete, the AI system may perpetuate or even exacerbate existing social inequalities. As professionals and innovators, it is important to be vigilant in identifying and mitigating bias in AI systems to ensure fair and equitable outcomes for all users.

Another ethical consideration in the development of advanced AI technologies is the issue of transparency and accountability. As AI systems become more complex and autonomous, it can be difficult to understand how they arrive at their decisions or to hold them accountable for their actions. Professionals and innovators must work to develop AI systems that are transparent and accountable, with clear mechanisms for explaining their decisions and processes.

Privacy and data security are also significant ethical concerns in the realm of advanced AI technologies. As AI systems collect and analyze vast amounts of personal data, there is a risk of privacy violations and breaches of data security. Professionals and innovators must prioritize the protection of user data and ensure that AI systems are designed and implemented in a way that respects user privacy and maintains data security.

Finally, the ethical implications of advanced AI technologies extend to broader societal impacts, such as job displacement and economic inequality. As AI systems automate tasks and processes previously performed by humans, there is a risk of widespread job loss and economic disruption. Professionals and innovators must consider the social and economic implications of AI technologies and work to mitigate potential negative impacts through policies and regulations that prioritize human welfare and well-being. By addressing these ethical implications of advanced AI technologies, professionals and innovators can help to ensure that AI technologies are developed and deployed in a way that benefits society as a whole.

Ethics of AI in Society

In today's rapidly evolving technological landscape, the integration of artificial intelligence (AI) into society has become increasingly prevalent. As professionals and innovators in the field of AI, it is essential to consider the ethical implications of this technology on society as a whole. The ethics of AI in society encompass a wide range of considerations, from privacy and data protection to bias and discrimination. It is crucial for professionals and innovators to navigate these ethical challenges with careful consideration and thoughtful decision-making.

One of the key ethical considerations in the use of AI in society is the issue of privacy and data protection. As AI systems become more sophisticated and integrated into various aspects of daily life, the collection and analysis of personal data have become commonplace. Professionals and innovators must ensure that they are taking appropriate measures to protect the privacy and security of individuals' data, while also being transparent about how that data is being used.

Another important ethical consideration in the use of AI in society is the issue of bias and discrimination. AI systems are often trained on data sets that may contain biases, leading to the potential for discriminatory outcomes. Professionals and innovators must work to identify and mitigate these biases in order to ensure that AI systems are fair and equitable for all individuals. This may involve implementing algorithms that are designed to minimize bias, as well as regularly monitoring and evaluating the performance of AI systems to ensure that they are not perpetuating discriminatory practices.

Additionally, professionals and innovators in the field of AI must consider the potential impact of their technology on society as a whole. This includes thinking about how AI systems may affect jobs and economic inequality, as well as the broader societal implications of widespread AI adoption. It is important for professionals and innovators to engage in thoughtful dialogue with stakeholders and policymakers to ensure that AI is being used in a way that benefits society as a whole.

Overall, the ethics of AI in society are complex and multifaceted, requiring careful consideration and thoughtful decision-making from professionals and innovators in the field. By approaching these ethical challenges with a commitment to transparency, fairness, and accountability, professionals and innovators can help to ensure that AI is being used in a way that benefits society as a whole.

Chapter 8: Conclusion and Recommendations
Summary of Key Points

In this subchapter, we have summarized the key points discussed throughout the book "Navigating the Ethical Landscape of AI: A Guide for Professionals and Innovators." As professionals and innovators in the field of AI ethics and regulation, it is crucial to understand the ethical implications of artificial intelligence and how to navigate the complex landscape of AI development.

The first key point to consider is the importance of ethical frameworks in AI development. Ethics should be at the forefront of decision-making processes when designing and implementing AI technologies. This includes considering the potential impact on society, privacy, and human rights. By incorporating ethical considerations into the development process, professionals can ensure that AI technologies are being used responsibly and ethically.

Secondly, it is essential to address bias and fairness in AI systems. Bias can be unintentionally introduced into AI algorithms, leading to discriminatory outcomes. Professionals and innovators must actively work to identify and mitigate bias in AI systems to ensure that they are fair and equitable for all users. This includes implementing measures such as bias detection tools, diverse datasets, and regular audits of AI systems.

Another key point is the importance of transparency and accountability in AI development. Professionals should strive to create transparent AI systems that are explainable and accountable for their decisions. This includes documenting the development process, providing explanations for AI decisions, and establishing mechanisms for accountability and redress when things go wrong. Transparency and accountability are essential for building trust with users and stakeholders.

Furthermore, it is crucial to consider the implications of AI on privacy and data protection. As professionals and innovators in the field of AI ethics and regulation, it is important to prioritize privacy and data protection in the design and implementation of AI technologies. This includes complying with data protection regulations, implementing privacy-enhancing technologies, and obtaining informed consent from users before collecting and processing their data.

In conclusion, navigating the ethical landscape of AI requires a deep understanding of the ethical implications of artificial intelligence and a commitment to responsible and ethical development practices. By incorporating ethical frameworks, addressing bias and fairness, prioritizing transparency and accountability, and considering privacy and data protection, professionals and innovators can ensure that AI technologies are developed and used in a responsible and ethical manner.

Recommendations for Practicing Ethical AI

As professionals and innovators in the field of AI ethics and regulation, it is crucial to adhere to ethical principles when developing and implementing artificial intelligence technologies. In order to ensure that

AI systems are used responsibly and ethically, it is important to follow certain recommendations for practicing ethical AI.

First and foremost, it is essential to prioritize transparency and accountability in AI systems. This means being open about how AI algorithms are designed and implemented, as well as taking responsibility for the outcomes of AI decisions. By ensuring transparency and accountability, professionals can build trust with users and stakeholders and mitigate potential risks associated with AI technologies.

Secondly, professionals and innovators should prioritize fairness and equity in AI systems. This involves ensuring that AI algorithms do not perpetuate biases or discriminate against certain groups of people. By incorporating fairness and equity into the design and implementation of AI systems, professionals can help create a more inclusive and just society.

Additionally, it is important to prioritize privacy and data protection when developing AI technologies. Professionals should be mindful of the personal data that AI systems collect and use, and take steps to protect the privacy and security of this data. By prioritizing privacy and data protection, professionals can build trust with users and ensure that AI technologies are used in a responsible and ethical manner.

Furthermore, professionals and innovators should prioritize human oversight and control in AI systems. This means ensuring that humans have the ability to intervene in AI decisions and override automated processes when necessary. By prioritizing human oversight and control, professionals can prevent AI systems from making harmful or unethical decisions and ensure that technology serves human interests.

In conclusion, by following these recommendations for practicing ethical AI, professionals and innovators can help ensure that AI technologies are used responsibly and ethically. By prioritizing transparency, fairness, privacy, and human oversight in AI systems, professionals can build trust with users, mitigate risks, and contribute to a more ethical and sustainable future for AI technology.

Continuing Education in AI Ethics for Professionals

Continuing education in AI ethics is crucial for professionals and innovators working in the field of artificial intelligence. As technology evolves rapidly, it is important for individuals to stay informed about the ethical implications of their work. By participating in ongoing education and training programs, professionals can ensure that they are equipped to make ethical decisions in their roles.

One key aspect of continuing education in AI ethics is staying up-to-date on the latest regulations and guidelines. As governments around the world develop new laws and policies related to AI, professionals must understand how these regulations impact their work. By staying informed about legal requirements, professionals can ensure that they are operating within the bounds of the law and avoid potential ethical pitfalls.

In addition to legal regulations, professionals should also be aware of best practices and ethical guidelines in the field of AI. This includes understanding principles such as transparency, accountability, and fairness in AI systems. By incorporating these principles into their work, professionals can ensure that their projects are ethically sound and have a positive impact on society.

Continuing education in AI ethics can take many forms, including workshops, seminars, and online courses. Professionals should take advantage of these opportunities to deepen their understanding of ethical issues in AI and develop the skills needed to make ethical decisions in their work. By investing in ongoing education, professionals can demonstrate their commitment to ethical practices and contribute to a more responsible and sustainable AI industry.

In conclusion, continuing education in AI ethics is essential for professionals and innovators working in the field of artificial intelligence. By staying informed about regulations, guidelines, and best practices, individuals can ensure that they are making ethical decisions in their work. By investing in ongoing education and training, professionals can contribute to a more responsible and sustainable AI industry that benefits society as a whole.

AI Ethics & Regulations Terms

Bias: Refers to the prejudices or unfair tendencies that can be introduced into AI systems through data, algorithms, or human decisions, leading to discriminatory outcomes.

Transparency: The principle that the operations and decisions of AI systems should be explainable and understandable to users and stakeholders.

Accountability: The requirement that entities involved in the development and deployment of AI systems are responsible for their impacts and outcomes.

Fairness: Ensuring that AI systems operate without favoritism or discrimination and provide equitable outcomes for all users.

Privacy: The protection of individuals' personal data and information from unauthorized access and misuse by AI systems.

Explainability: The extent to which the internal mechanisms of an AI system can be understood and interpreted by humans.

Autonomy: The ability of AI systems to perform tasks and make decisions without human intervention.

Safety: Ensuring that AI systems do not cause harm to humans and operate within safe boundaries.

Ethical AI: The development and deployment of AI systems in a manner that aligns with ethical principles and societal values.

Regulation: Legal frameworks and guidelines governing the development, deployment, and use of AI technologies to ensure they are safe, fair, and ethical.

Data Protection: Measures and practices to safeguard personal data used by AI systems, ensuring compliance with privacy laws and regulations.

Algorithmic Transparency: The disclosure of how algorithms function and make decisions, to ensure they are free from bias and can be trusted.

Consent: The requirement that individuals are informed and agree to the use of their data in AI systems.

Human-in-the-Loop (HITL): A model where human judgment is incorporated into the decision-making process of AI systems, ensuring oversight and control.

Ethical Guidelines: Frameworks and principles designed to guide the ethical development and use of AI technologies.

Adversarial Attacks: Attempts to deceive or manipulate AI systems by providing misleading input, potentially causing them to malfunction.

Machine Learning Fairness: Techniques and practices aimed at reducing bias and ensuring equitable outcomes in machine learning models.

Deepfake: Synthetic media created using AI that can convincingly replace the likeness of one person with another in video or audio.

AI Governance: The policies, procedures, and structures put in place to ensure that AI development and deployment align with ethical standards and regulations.

AI Auditing: The process of reviewing and evaluating AI systems to ensure they meet ethical standards and regulatory requirements.

AI Regulations Around the World

1. European Union - General Data Protection Regulation (GDPR)

Description: Enacted in 2018, GDPR is one of the most comprehensive data protection regulations in the world. It applies to all companies processing the personal data of individuals residing in the EU, regardless of the company's location. GDPR includes provisions that impact AI, such as the right to explanation for automated decisions, data minimization, and consent for data processing.

2. European Union - Artificial Intelligence Act (Proposed)

Description: The AI Act, proposed in 2021, aims to establish a framework for the development, deployment, and use of AI in the EU. It categorizes AI applications into four risk levels: unacceptable, high, limited, and minimal. High-risk AI systems will be subject to stringent requirements, including risk management, data governance, and human oversight.

3. United States - Algorithmic Accountability Act (Proposed)

Description: Proposed in 2019, this Act would require companies to conduct impact assessments for automated decision systems to identify and mitigate potential biases and risks. It focuses on the transparency and accountability of algorithms, especially those used in critical areas like healthcare, employment, and finance.

4. China - New Generation Artificial Intelligence Development Plan

Description: Launched in 2017, this plan outlines China's strategy to become a global leader in AI by 2030. It includes goals for AI research, development, and ethical guidelines. The plan emphasizes the importance of AI security, ethics, and the establishment of laws and regulations to guide AI development.

5. Canada - Directive on Automated Decision-Making

Description: Implemented in 2019, this directive sets requirements for the federal government's use of automated decision systems. It mandates impact assessments, transparency, and the establishment of mechanisms for human intervention. The directive aims to ensure fairness, accountability, and transparency in government use of AI.

6. Singapore - Model AI Governance Framework

Description: Released in 2019 by the Infocomm Media Development Authority (IMDA) and the Personal Data Protection Commission (PDPC), this framework provides detailed guidance on AI governance. It covers areas like internal governance structures, risk management, operations management, and stakeholder interaction, aiming to promote ethical and responsible use of AI.

7. Japan - Social Principles of Human-centric AI

Description: Adopted in 2019, Japan's AI principles focus on promoting human-centric AI development. They emphasize respect for human dignity, privacy, and the promotion of fairness, transparency, and accountability. The principles serve as a foundation for Japan's AI policies and regulations.

8. Australia - AI Ethics Framework

Description: Published in 2019, this framework provides eight principles to guide the ethical development and use of AI in Australia. The principles include human, social, and environmental wellbeing, human-centered values, fairness, privacy protection, reliability and safety, transparency and explainability, contestability, and accountability.

9. South Korea - National Strategy for Artificial Intelligence

Description: Announced in 2019, this strategy aims to position South Korea as a global AI leader by 2030. It includes initiatives for AI research, industry support, and ethical guidelines. The strategy emphasizes the importance of AI ethics, safety, and the establishment of legal and regulatory frameworks.

10. United Kingdom - AI Sector Deal

Description: Part of the UK's Industrial Strategy, the AI Sector Deal was launched in 2018. It outlines the UK's approach to AI development, focusing on investment in AI research, skills, and ethical standards. The deal includes commitments to developing AI regulations that ensure safety, fairness, and transparency.

Top Countries Leading in AI Development, Research, And Implementation

The top countries leading in AI development, research, and implementation are recognized for their significant contributions to the field, strong AI ecosystems, and supportive government policies. Here's a list of some of the top AI countries in the world:

United States

- The US is a global leader in AI research, innovation, and commercialization. It is home to major tech companies like Google, Microsoft, IBM, and Amazon, which invest heavily in AI. The US also has numerous top-ranked universities and research institutions contributing to AI advancements.

China

- China has made AI a national priority with its "New Generation Artificial Intelligence Development Plan" aiming to become the world leader in AI by 2030. The country has massive investments in AI, supported by both the government and private sector giants like Baidu, Alibaba, and Tencent.

United Kingdom

- The UK is known for its strong AI research community and robust AI ecosystem. It has established policies and strategies, such as the AI Sector Deal, to promote AI development. The country is home to leading AI companies and research institutions.

Canada

- Canada is recognized for its pioneering AI research and is home to leading AI hubs in Toronto, Montreal, and Edmonton. The country has a strong emphasis on ethical AI and has produced many influential AI researchers and entrepreneurs.

Germany

- Germany has a strong focus on AI in industrial applications, particularly in manufacturing and automotive sectors. The country has invested in AI research and development through initiatives like the AI Made in Germany strategy, and it has a robust network of AI startups and research institutions.

France

- France is actively investing in AI through its national AI strategy, which aims to foster innovation and research. The country is home to several leading AI research centers and companies, and it emphasizes ethical AI development.

Japan

- Japan is a leader in AI, especially in robotics and industrial applications. The country's "Society 5.0" initiative aims to integrate AI and other advanced technologies into all aspects of society. Japan has a strong research community and is known for its innovation in AI and robotics.

South Korea

- South Korea is heavily investing in AI to drive economic growth and innovation. The country's National Strategy for Artificial Intelligence aims to make South Korea a global AI leader by 2030. It has a strong tech industry and supportive government policies for AI development.

Singapore

- Singapore has established itself as an AI hub in Asia with its strategic investments and initiatives, such as the AI Singapore program. The country focuses on AI governance and ethics and has a thriving AI ecosystem supported by government and private sector collaboration.

Israel

- Israel is known for its vibrant tech startup ecosystem and significant contributions to AI research and development. The country has a strong focus on innovation and has produced many successful AI startups and technologies.

AI Ethical Frameworks from Around the World

IEEE - Ethically Aligned Design (EAD)

- **Description:** Developed by the IEEE Global Initiative on Ethics of Autonomous and Intelligent Systems, EAD provides guidelines for designing AI systems that prioritize human well-being and ethical principles. It includes recommendations on transparency, accountability, and privacy.

2. EU High-Level Expert Group on AI - Ethics Guidelines for Trustworthy AI

- **Description:** These guidelines focus on ensuring AI is lawful, ethical, and robust. They outline seven key requirements for trustworthy AI: human agency and oversight, technical robustness and safety, privacy and data governance, transparency, diversity and fairness, societal and environmental well-being, and accountability.

3. OECD - AI Principles

- **Description:** The Organization for Economic Cooperation and Development (OECD) has established five principles to guide AI development: inclusive growth, sustainable development and well-being; human-centered values and fairness; transparency and explainability; robustness, security, and safety; and accountability.

4. Singapore - Model AI Governance Framework

- **Description:** This framework offers practical guidance to organizations on how to deploy AI responsibly. It covers internal governance structures, risk management, operations management, and stakeholder interaction, emphasizing transparency, accountability, and fairness.

5. Google - AI Principles

- **Description:** Google's AI principles outline the company's commitment to developing AI technologies responsibly. These principles include being socially beneficial, avoiding creating or reinforcing bias, being accountable, incorporating privacy design, and ensuring AI technologies are used for purposes that align with these principles.

6. Microsoft - Responsible AI Principles

- **Description:** Microsoft's framework focuses on six principles: fairness, reliability and safety, privacy and security, inclusiveness, transparency, and accountability. These principles guide the development and deployment of AI technologies within the company.

7. IBM - AI Ethics for AI

- **Description:** IBM's AI ethics framework emphasizes transparency, explainability, fairness, robustness, privacy, and accountability. The company is committed to developing AI that augments human intelligence and addresses social challenges.

8. Canada - Directive on Automated Decision-Making

- **Description:** This directive sets out requirements for the use of automated decision systems in the federal government, including impact assessments, transparency, and mechanisms for human intervention, focusing on fairness, accountability, and transparency.

9. Japan - Social Principles of Human-centric AI

- **Description:** Japan's principles emphasize the importance of human dignity, privacy, and promoting fairness, transparency, and accountability in AI development and deployment, aiming for AI that benefits society.

10. Australian Government - AI Ethics Principles

- **Description:** These principles provide a framework for the ethical development and use of AI in Australia. They include human, social, and environmental well-being, human-centered values, fairness, privacy protection, reliability and safety, transparency and explainability, contestability, and accountability.

11. World Economic Forum - AI Ethics and Governance Guidelines

- **Description:** These guidelines offer a global perspective on ethical AI, focusing on principles like human-centric AI, transparency, accountability, and privacy. They aim to foster global cooperation and responsible AI development.

12. AI4People - Ethical Framework for a Good AI Society

- **Description:** AI4People's framework is based on four ethical principles: beneficence (promoting well-being, preserving dignity), non-maleficence (avoiding harm), autonomy (preserving human agency), and justice (promoting fairness). It provides a comprehensive approach to ethical AI.